DETECTING DISASTERS

DETECTING WILDFIRES

by Samantha S. Bell

FOCUS READERS

WWW.NORTHSTAREDITIONS.COM

Produced for North Star Editions by Red Line Editorial.

Photographs ©: Digital Media Pro/Shutterstock Images, cover, 1; Jae C. Hong/AP Images, 4–5; Shutterstock Images, 6, 9, 10–11, 13, 14, 19; North Wind Picture Archives, 16–17; Berni Schoenfield/Hulton Archive/Getty Images, 21; Keystone-France/Getty Images, 22–23; danlogan/iStockphoto, 24–25; NASA, 27; Pierre Andrieu/AFP/Getty Images, 28

Content Consultant: Sen Chiao, PhD, Associate Professor, Meteorology and Climate Science, San José State University

ISBN
978-1-63517-007-8 (hardcover)
978-1-63517-063-4 (paperback)
978-1-63517-169-3 (ebook pdf)
978-1-63517-119-8 (hosted ebook)

Library of Congress Control Number: 2016949753

Printed in the United States of America
Mankato, MN
November, 2016

ABOUT THE AUTHOR

Samantha S. Bell lives with her family and lots of pets in the foothills of South Carolina. She loves writing about nature, and she is the author or illustrator of more than 60 books for children.

TABLE OF CONTENTS

CHAPTER 1

THE RIM FIRE

On August 17, 2013, a man was hunting deer in California's Stanislaus National Forest. The area was very dry, and signs stated no campfires were allowed. But the hunter disobeyed the signs. He decided to start a fire to cook some beans. Embers flew into nearby plants. Leaves and grasses sparked and began to ignite.

It took firefighters months to fully contain the fire that started in August 2013.

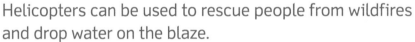

Helicopters can be used to rescue people from wildfires and drop water on the blaze.

Twigs and branches crackled, and flames leaped from tree to tree. Before the hunter could stop it, the fire was out of control.

Someone saw the smoke from the fire and reported it. A fire helicopter flew to the scene. The crew found the hunter and brought him back to safety. Meanwhile, officials planned how to fight the fire. By the time they decided what to do, the fire covered 150 acres (61 ha). And it raged on, lighting up the forest as it burned.

MEGAFIRES

Some wildfires are called megafires. These are huge, intense fires on public land. They are mostly in the western United States, although other countries also have megafires. These fires often burn in areas where wood, **brush**, and other fuels have built up. A dry **climate** helps megafires spread quickly.

In less than three weeks, it became the third-largest fire in California's history.

The blaze became known as the Rim Fire because it started near a scenic point called Rim of the World. The Rim Fire burned for four months. By the time firefighters were able to put it out, it had burned 256,000 acres (103,600 ha) of Stanislaus National Forest and Yosemite National Park.

The fire destroyed wildlife habitats, killed livestock, and destroyed more than 100 buildings. But amazingly, only 10 people were injured, and none were killed. Soon after the fire started, officials helped get campers to safety. Within

Two years after the Rim Fire, the wildfire's impact could still be seen.

days, whole towns were **evacuated**. Even though the fire could not be controlled, early detection saved many lives.

CHAPTER 2

WHAT IS A WILDFIRE?

Wildfires are also called wildland fires or forest fires. They occur on every continent except Antarctica. These fires burn in brush, forests, and grasslands. Every year in the United States, there are more than 100,000 wildfires.

With wind and dry weather, wildfires can double in size every five minutes.

Wildfires can last for weeks or even months.

These fires can quickly spread and destroy everything in their paths.

Most wildfires are caused by people. They may leave campfires unattended. They may burn trash or throw used cigarettes on the ground. Occasionally, people start fires on purpose.

Sometimes natural events cause wildfires. Lightning can trigger destructive fires. If a storm knocks over power lines, a spark can start a fire, too.

A wildfire needs oxygen, heat, and fuel. The oxygen comes from the air. The heat comes from fires started by people or nature. The fuel is any material that can burn, such as plants, branches, leaves,

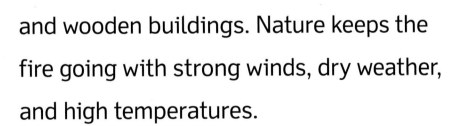

Lightning is sometimes responsible for starting wildfires.

and wooden buildings. Nature keeps the fire going with strong winds, dry weather, and high temperatures.

Wildfires can hurt not only people but also the environment. They pollute the atmosphere with harmful haze and smoke.

Natural wildfires are often healthy for a forest.

Carbon dioxide and other **greenhouse gases** are released into the air. Wildfires burn homes, businesses, and the land where people make their livings. They destroy wildlife habitats and cause soil erosion.

Fire is not always harmful. Sometimes it actually helps the land. The burned plants provide nutrients for the soil. Clearing away trees opens up the **forest floor** to sunlight. This helps other trees grow stronger and healthier.

TYPES OF WILDFIRES

Wildfires are classified into three different categories. Ground fires burn matter in the soil below the forest floor. They are usually started by lightning. Surface fires are the most common. They burn slowly along the forest floor, damaging or killing the trees. Crown fires burn through the tops of trees. They spread quickly in high winds and are often the hardest to contain.

CHAPTER 3

EARLY WARNING SYSTEMS

The US government created the United States Forest Service in 1905. Its policy was to put out wildfires no matter the size or threat. But during the summer of 1910, there were more fires than the Forest Service could handle.

The fires killed 85 people and burned 3 million acres (1.2 million ha) of **timber**.

Before the 1930s, there was often little warning of deadly forest fires.

Fire detection became a priority. To help spot wildfires, the government built lookout towers on mountaintops in national forests throughout the United States.

THE FIRST WOMAN LOOKOUT

In 1913, Hallie M. Daggett started working at a lookout station on Klamath Peak in the Klamath National Forest. This forest is on the border of California and Oregon. Every summer for 15 years, she sat alone in the tower, watching for fires. Her sister would bring supplies and mail once a week. Hallie did not mind the storms or the wild animals. She enjoyed the job and was happy to join the fight against wildfires.

Lookouts often lived in their towers for weeks at a time.

Early fire spotters used the Osborne Firefinder, a device created in 1911 by William Bushnell Osborne Jr. By sighting distant smoke in the Firefinder, spotters could determine the location of a forest fire. Firefinders are still used today throughout the world.

Rural telephones also helped officials detect wildfires. The Forest Service's first telephone line was constructed in 1906 in Wyoming. Telephones provided better communication for spotters and forest rangers.

Just after World War I (1914–1918), the Forest Service joined with the Army Air Service to provide airplanes and pilots to spot wildfires from the air. The program worked well for more than 10 years. By the 1930s, a large system of lookout towers and telephones was ready to take its place.

Spotting fires from lookout towers usually works well. But a spotter's view

Ground crews worked with pilots in the air to track wildfires.

can be limited by clouds or fog. And watching for fires for days at a time can be boring and tiring. Today, only a few hundred lookout stations are still used in the United States.

OSBORNE FIREFINDER

The Osborne Firefinder looks like a round glass table with a map underneath it. The map shows the surrounding land. The lookout tower is in the center. Along the outside are two rings. The top ring has two sights for the spotter to look through. It spins around the map. The other ring has numbers and stays in place. Spotters line up the two sights with the smoke they see. A measuring tape between the two sights helps the spotter estimate how far away it is. The elevation can be found by using the measurements on a sliding piece on the rear sight.

The Osborne Firefinder is one type of alidade, a kind of device used to spot and measure distant objects.

rear sight

local map

handle for turning

front sight

rotating ring

CHAPTER 4

MODERN METHODS

Improvements in technology have led to advanced new systems for detecting wildfires. Some of these systems use video cameras. The cameras are usually mounted on a tower close to a potential fire source. These cameras can detect smoke and fire within the surrounding 116 square miles (300 sq km).

Some lookout towers now have cameras mounted on them.

Some cameras have sensors that estimate the location, size, speed, and direction of the fire.

Wildfires are still detected from above, too. Spotters in modern planes look for fires. The higher the planes go, the larger the area the spotters can search. **Satellite** systems cover even wider areas.

In 2015, forestry officials also began using **drones** to detect wildfires. The first one was used during the Paradise Fire in Washington's Olympic National Park. The drone gathered information when conditions were too smoky to use piloted airplanes. The drone used **infrared** technology to find how widely the fire

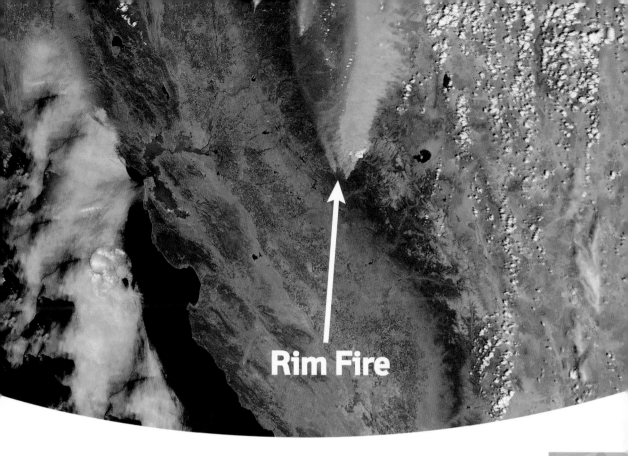

Rim Fire

Smoke from the Rim Fire could be seen by satellites.

had spread and where the heat was most intense.

Early detection is important when fighting wildfires. When officials know the location, strength, and speed of a fire, they can make better decisions.

Firefighters in France test a drone that will be used to track wildfires.

Officials need to find out whether people will be in danger. They must determine if the fire is small enough to manage or if they should try to put it out. They know that the larger a wildfire grows before it is detected, the harder it is to fight.

WILDFIRE SAFETY CHECKLIST

- Know if you are in an area that is at risk of wildfires.

- Prepare an emergency kit with a flashlight, batteries, money, and first aid supplies.

- Prepare your home in case a wildfire comes near. Clean the roof and gutters regularly. Make sure to clear away objects that could burn, such as piles of wood or brush.

- If you see a wildfire and have not received evacuation orders yet, call 911. Don't assume another person has already called it in.

- Listen to the radio and watch the television for news and emergency instructions.

- If you are ordered to evacuate, make sure to tell someone where you and your family are going.

- If you get burned by the fire, call 911 or find medical help quickly. Cool the burn with clean running water, and cover it to prevent infections.

- Return home only after the authorities declare your area safe.

FOCUS ON
DETECTING WILDFIRES

Write your answers on a separate piece of paper.

1. Write a paragraph outlining the major ways in which people detect wildfires.

2. Would you want to work in a wildfire lookout tower? Why or why not?

3. Which wildfire detecting devices are used in lookout towers?

>   **A.** Osborne Firefinders
>   **B.** drones
>   **C.** satellites

4. Why are drones with infrared technology useful for detecting fires?

>   **A.** People aboard can spot a fire.
>   **B.** The drones can detect heat.
>   **C.** The drones can predict where a fire might start.

Answer key on page 32.

GLOSSARY

brush
Short trees or shrubs.

climate
The weather conditions of a certain area over a long period of time.

drones
Remote-controlled aircraft without pilots.

evacuated
Removed people from a place of danger.

forest floor
The upper layer of soil and decaying matter in a forest.

greenhouse gases
Gases that trap heat in Earth's atmosphere, causing climate change.

infrared
Light that is invisible to human eyes but can be seen by certain cameras.

satellite
A device that orbits Earth.

timber
Trees grown for their wood.

TO LEARN MORE

BOOKS

Adamson, Thomas K., and Heather Adamson. *California Wildfires Survival Stories*. Mankato, MN: Child's World, 2016.

Thiessen, Mark. *Extreme Wildfire*. Washington, DC: National Geographic Children's Books, 2016.

Watts, Claire, and Trevor Day. *Natural Disasters*. New York: DK Children's Books, 2012.

NOTE TO EDUCATORS

Visit **www.focusreaders.com** to find lesson plans, activities, links, and other resources related to this title.

INDEX

Answer Key: 1. Answers will vary; **2.** Answers will vary; **3.** A; **4.** B